THE Umbrella UNFURLED

THE
Umbrella
UNFURLED

Its Remarkable Life and Times

Nigel Rodgers

BENE FACTUM PUBLISHING

The Umbrella Unfurled

First published in 2013 by
Bene Factum Publishing Ltd
PO Box 58122
London
SW8 5WZ
Email: inquiries@bene-factum.co.uk
www.bene-factum.co.uk

ISBN: 978-1-903071-68-7

A CIP catalogue record of this is available from the British Library

Book design by Mousemat Design Ltd
Printed edition printed and bound in Slovenia for Latitude Press
Cover design by Henry Rivers

Cover image: Shutwis / Shutterstock
Interior: Acclaim Images; Paul Almasy / CORBIS; The Bridgeman Art Library; Scott Stulberg / Corbis; Oranong / Shutterstock; Erich Lessing Culture and Fine Arts Archive; Victoria and Albert Museum, London; Bettmann / CORBIS; Luigi Nifosi / Shutterstock; Clipart courtesy FCIT; Mary Evans Picture Library / Alamy; The National Gallery, London. Bought, Courtauld Fund, 1924; Museum of London, UK / The Bridgeman Art Library; John Leech Archive; Mike Roche; Getty Images; SuperStock / Alamy; Swim Ink 2, LLC / CORBIS; Gil Elvgren; Robert Capa / International Center of Photography / Magnum Photos; Galerie Bilderwelt / The Bridgeman Art Library; Fox Umbrellas; James Smith & Sons Umbrellas Ltd; Kevin McGarry / Lansdowne Club; Parasolerie Heurtault; Maglia Umbrella Company; Pasotti Ombrelli; Roulier / Turiot / photocuisine / Corbis

Good housewives all the winter's rage despise,
Defended by the riding-hood's disguise;
Or, underneath the umbrella's oily shade,
Safe through the wet on clinking pattens tread,
Let Persian dames the umbrella's ribs display,
To guard their beauties from the sunny ray;
Or sweating slaves support the shady load,
When eastern monarchs show their state abroad;
Britain in winter only knows its aid,
To guard from chilling showers the walking maid.
John Gay, 1685-1732

Acknowledgements

Among the many people who have helped with suggestions, ideas and images, I am especially indebted to the following:

Raj Jayawadena and Anthony Livesey who supplied the Ghanaian photograph; Kevin McGarry who photographed the mural from the Lansdowne Club; and Carolyn Rodgers for all her sage advice.

I am again grateful to the tirelessly helpful staff of the London Library; also to the British Library and the Victoria & Albert National Art Library.

Finally, my thanks to Dominic Horsfall for all his fine editing.

Nigel Rodgers, London and Wiltshire, 2013

Contents

William D. Upshaw, an American Congressman of the early 20th century, and a strong advocate of temperance and prohibition, raises his umbrella symbolically over the Capitol to keep the country 'dry'.

A Brief History of the Brolly

'All men are equal – all men, that is to say,
who possess umbrellas.'
E. M Forster 1879-1970

Umbrella: the word means merely 'little shade' but the object casts a long shadow. From ancient Egypt and India to modern Miami, via China, Africa, Paris, London and New York, the umbrella and its silkier sister the parasol have shielded, decorated and delighted humanity. Whether in black or every colour of the carnival, umbrellas and parasols give at least the illusion of shelter against the elements. They are in fact the earliest and smallest versions of the *mobile home.*

Mobility is the vital word. Mobility distinguishes every umbrella and parasol from fixed tents or awnings. Umbrellas and parasols accompany their carriers through thick and thin. In doing so they become as personal, colourful and idiosyncratic as hats or gloves – all items with surprising erotic potential.

The umbrella has also made solemn panoplies to support the dignity of rajahs, popes, emperors, sultans and kings. In the 17th century Moulay Ismaïl Ibn Sharif, Sultan of Morocco, had an umbrella 11ft (3.5m) high topped by a gilt cockerel, surpassing even the ornate umbrellas of Louis XIV, his French contemporary. The pope still has a grandiose papal umbrella to enhance pontifical power.

In sober contrast, the first famous desert island castaway, Robinson Crusoe, 'spent a great deal of time and pain to make an

Above: Two girls cycle past with their parasols proudly displayed during the procession at the hugely colourful Bo Sang Umbrella Festival, held every year in Chiang Mai Province, Thailand.
Below: During the festival the village comes to life. Festivities include the Miss Bo Sang beauty pageant, the winner no doubt being chosen no doubt chosen for the quality of her brolly.

umbrella' which doubled as a parasol. By 1719, the year the novel appeared, an umbrella was considered essential to civilised survival, although it was still a comparative rarity on the streets of London.

To see the umbrella as simply a way of keeping off the rain, a drab black item held aloft by those scurrying to work, underrates its global and historical importance. It has starred on screen and stage and, especially in the form of the parasol, been invaluable in flirtation. It has gone to war, being used to protect military uniforms – in the days when these were worth protecting – and as a weapon itself. (The umbrella-swordstick: very lethal.) It has even been used in aviation: catastrophically on a few occasions as a parachute, or once more successfully to lift a governess high above the roofs of London.

'Umbrella' is derived from Italian *ombrella,* little shade, and ultimately from Latin *umbra,* shadow. 'Parasol' comes from the Italian *parasole,* protection against the sun. The French call the two *parapluie*, against rain, and, confusingly, *ombrelle*. The Germans more logically use the words *Regenschirm* and *Sonnenschirm*, rain/sun shields.

Like gloves and hats, parasols and umbrellas have at times been declared redundant – superfluous ornaments in a clean-cut modern world. But they have always resurfaced, often in wittier, more elegant forms than ever. For umbrellas and parasols are both decorative *and* functional, to be celebrated and carried whatever the weather, as their joint history shows.

A priest holds the cross of Christianity while shielding himself from the hot Ethiopian sun near Lake Tana. Note the contrast of the pragmatic, earthly brolly with the ecclesiastical splendour of his priestly robe.

CHAPTER ONE

The Dawn of the Umbrella

In the beginning was the parasol. Lighter than the umbrella, the parasol precedes its bulkier brother by millennia, for the sun's rays are stopped even by the flimsiest of shelters. To distinguish between the two in early times is pointless anyway. Today, the same objects function in India as both umbrella and sunshade, depending on weather.

The parasol was first seen in ancient Egypt, the Middle East, India and China. Carried solemnly in victory parades or religious rites, it exalted the majesty and divinity of gods, god-kings and high priests. Normally it was carried by slaves or servants, for these early sunshades were large, heavy, highly decorated artefacts.

In Egypt parasols initially sheltered only the pharaoh's head. There was a religious element behind such exclusivity. The Egyptians believed that the sky-goddess Nut shielded humanity by arching her star-spangled body over the night sky, only her toes and fingertips touching the earth. When they raised up their parasols, ancient Egyptians were partly trying to emulate their maternal goddess's protection. A grand parasol above the pharaoh stressed his divinity and power. To 'fall under the pharaoh's shadow' meant falling under his power.

The Egyptian sun itself, however, was good enough reason for seeking shade. The privilege and comfort of being shaded gradually filtered down to the rest of the court. Wall paintings of around 1200BC from tombs in Thebes (Luxor) show princesses or court ladies driving in elegant little two-horse chariots with fringed sunshades. Such early parasols may have been made of leaves or linen, with bamboo or similar ribs. Fragile objects, they were not designed to repel rain. But it hardly ever rains in Upper Egypt.

The royal parasol fashion spread. In alabaster reliefs dating to c.650BC from an Assyrian palace at Nineveh, now in Iraq, King Ashurbanipal is shown taking part in a military procession. A slave or a courtier just behind him is holding a sunshade to shield the king in his chariot. This parasol appears to have been an exceptionally hefty object. Its long thick pole required both hands to support it, while a heavy linen flap hanging behind it and tassels around its base gave almost all-round shelter. In short, no dainty sunshade but a power-parasol.

As such it suited the ruler of the world's first superpower whose war chariots had carved out an empire stretching from Egypt to Iran, crushing in their path peoples such as the Israelites. However Ashurbanipal, also famed as the first monarch to have founded a library, was the last of his dynasty to rule a great kingdom. It collapsed soon afterwards, Nineveh falling to the combined attacks of the Babylonians and Persians. What happened to the royal parasol remains unknown.

The Persians, the heirs of Ashurbanipal's imperialism, also inherited the custom of using parasols as regal props. According to the Athenian historian Xenophon in his history *Cyropedia* (Boyhood of Cyrus), written c.380BC, Persian royalty and nobles made use of elaborate parasols against the sun's heat. King Xerxes I is depicted in about 480BC on a ceremonial gate at Persepolis, the ceremonial capital, a solemn procession of one under a parasol. In another carving, he is shown receiving tributaries and courtiers. Above him are two young slaves. One holds a parasol over the royal head while another wields what looks like a fly whisk. (Zoroastrian Persians had a particular abhorrence of flies, regarding them as emissaries of Satan.)

King Xerxes, portrayed on the side of a gateway in Persepolis, the Persian capital, in a solemn procession of one under his power-parasol c. 480BC. Such parasols were then an essential accessory for any Middle Eastern monarch.

In India the umbrella has been linked with power, prestige and religion for more than 3000 years. Typical of such power-parasols was the nava-danda. This had seven tiers of scarlet and gold cloth covered with 32 strings of pearls, a frame of pure gold and a handle made of a ruby with a diamond knob. It was deemed   suitable only for monarchs on grand occasions such as coronations. Little wonder that the Mogul rulers of India in the 16th and 17th centuries restricted the use of such sunshields to their own dynasty. Nobles had to be content with a white parasol with gold fringes.

The ancient Persian name for provincial governor *sattrapas* (satrap) may be the origin of Ch'hatra-pati, Lord of the Umbrella, a title assumed by later rulers in India such as the Mahratta princes of Punah and Sattara. A Maharajah of Nagpur had a ceremonial umbrella with sixteen ribs covered in silk and adorned with silver and gold decorations. This mighty sunshade was shown at the Great Exhibition in London in 1851. The ruler of Ova proudly called himself 'King of the White Elephant and Lord of the Twenty-Four Parasols'. The rajahs of Cochin even incorporated the outline of an umbrella in their postage stamps, so pervasive was Indian brollymania by the 19th century. Among the many titles of the kings of Burma in 1859 was 'Lord of the Great Parasol'.

In 1638 the German traveller Johann Albrecht von Mandelsloh noted the widespread Indian use of ceremonial parasols. 'No one who thinks himself a person of any importance in Goa appears on foot in the street but has himself carried by slaves in a palanquin with a great *quitesol* or sunshade to protect him from the sun's heat and also for pomp and show', he wrote. As the British began settling in southern India in the late 17th century, they adopted the ceremonial use of the parasol/umbrella, then little known in Britain. In 1687 in Madras (Chennai) aldermen of the Madras Corporation were permitted to carry *kettysols* (a variant of the Portuguese *quitesol*) to demonstrate their authority.

Pomp and ceremony long predominated in India under British rule. When Edward VII as Prince of Wales toured India in 1877 – the first British royal to do so – he rode an elephant beneath a vast golden parasol. Both were thought essential to uphold the royal status. The

Queen Mary, when visiting India in 1911 for the Grand Durbar to celebrate her husband King George V's accession to the throne, was accompanied by a turbaned attendant carrying an immense parasol. She was the only person to have such an honour.

prince returned home with 20 magnificent sunshades given to him by Indian rulers, some embroidered, others covered with feathers. The most luxurious, from the Begum of Oude, was made of blue silk stitched with gold thread and covered in pearls. The prince never found a use for these superb examples and they are now on display in the Victoria and Albert Museum in London.

However Queen Mary, the consort of Edward's son George V, when visiting India in 1911 for the grandiose durbar to celebrate the king's accession, was accompanied by a turbaned attendant carrying an elaborate parasol. Interestingly, Queen Mary alone had such a brolly-bearer. Other members of the royal retinue had to carry their parasols themselves. Umbrellas at the time certainly signalled status.

Mindful of the Enlightened One's example, Buddhist monks in Burma take their umbrellas/parasols everywhere, even into the monastery. The colours of their sunshades at times match those of their robes.

Perhaps the umbrella's noblest roles are in Hindu and Buddhist legend. Varuna, a deity associated with the sky and ocean, carried an umbrella called the Abhoga made from the hood of a cobra. The god Vishnu, in his fifth incarnation, borrowed Varuna's umbrella when he took on a pigmy's shape and descended into hell, escorted by umbrella-carrying Brahmins. In the ancient epic *Mahabharata* parasols are mentioned: 'The litter on which was placed the lifeless body of the monarch Pandou was adorned with a flywhisk, a fan and a parasol. As music played, hundreds of men offered... flywhisks and parasols.' Today the umbrella is still widely used in Hindu religious processions, sheltering or honouring the gods' statues.

The umbrella figures prominently in Buddhism too. The god

Brahma held a white umbrella over the new-born infant who would become the Enlightened One. At the end of the Buddha's life dark umbrellas sheltered his funeral procession. In early Buddhist carvings, where the Buddha himself is seldom shown, a parasol is sculpted over empty space or a prayer-wheel, indicating that the Buddha, if invisible, is still present. Under the Buddhist emperor Ashoka in the 3rd century BC, the novel shape of the stupa, the archetypal Buddhist structure, first appeared, in part inspired by umbrellas. Many stupas were even decorated with carved umbrellas or had umbrellas perched on top of them. On Buddhist sculptures from Gandhara of c.AD200, two types of parasol are discernible: one with a grand dome, the other shaped like a wheel.

In China the umbrella or San, the 'shade against sun and rain', had emerged by 1000BC independently of developments further west. It is mentioned in the *Rites of Tcheou* of the 11th century BC, which ordained that ceremonial chariots should be adorned with parasols made of silk or feathers with 28 curved ribs.

Early Chinese brolly technology seems to have been far more advanced than that of the west, for collapsible umbrella stays dating to about 25BC have been found in the tomb of the warlord Wang Kuang. Around the same time, the emperor Wang Mang's ceremonial chariot was protected by a *kui-kai*, a parasol that could be collapsed by a telescopic mechanism called a *pi-chi*. As protection against the rain was as important as shelter from the sun, the Chinese needed parasols/umbrellas to be robust and practical. Oiled paper and/or silk were used as water-repellent materials from earliest times, as they still are for some parasols and umbrellas.

Functionalism, however, was never central to the development of the umbrella in China any more than it was elsewhere. Instead, elaborate ceremony to demonstrate precise status was the thing. In imperial China the emperor was preceded by 24 parasol-bearers on grand occasions, while a four-tier gold silk sunshade covered in flowers, jewels

The umbrella figures so frequently in early Buddhist legends that the Buddha himself is at times shown carrying a brolly.

The Chinese seem to have had advanced umbrella technology from a very early time, for collapsible umbrella stays have been found in tombs dating back to 25BC. This elegant gentleman-scholar dates back even further to 1000BC.

20

Ceremonial chariots in ancient China had a *kui-kai*, a high-tech parasol collapsed by a telescopic mechanism called a *pi-chi*, as ordained in the *Rites of Tcheou* of the 11th century BC.

and feathers sheltered the head of Son of Heaven. An edict of 1012 restricting the use parasols to members of the imperial family was widely ignored. Finally under the Ming dynasty (1368-1644) the use of umbrellas was tightly regulated. A general or provincial governor was now heralded by two huge red silk umbrellas, for example.

'A Chinese of any rank at all, such as a mandarin or priest, never goes out without a parasol,' wrote Monsieur M. Cazal, a French brolly-maker and historian, in 1844. 'Every Chinese of the upper classes is attended by a servant who carries his parasol extended above him… Even their horses are sheltered by parasols.' (Cazal also noted that all Chinese umbrellas were made with simple bamboo ribs. Either Chinese brolly technology had regressed by his time or, more probably, he was allowed to examine only the simpler type of umbrella.)

A mandarin's rank could be discerned from whether his parasol had one, two or three tiers. The highest ranks of mandarins were given parasols of black *lo* (a form of Chinese gauze) with red silk linings and three tiers. All these umbrellas were made of dragon-embroidered silk. Minor officials and ordinary people could carry only umbrellas of oiled paper. An illustrious foreigner, such as the new German ambassador to the imperial court in 1897, might be given a single-tier red silk umbrella as a symbol of his (relatively modest) authority.

In Japan the parasol also played its part in outdoor ceremonies from early times. Tombs from the 5th century AD have yielded clay sculptures called *haniwa*, some of which depict parasols called *kinugasa*. These were insubstantial objects made of feathers and leaves with bamboo handles and ribs, almost certainly used to indicate the status of the dead. Although the Japanese did not give the umbrella the same solemn importance as the Chinese, umbrellas or sunshades called *naga-e* were held over the head of noblemen while

Three Japanese women using parasols or umbrellas against the snow, as painted by Utagawa Hiroshiga.

priests, courtiers and imperial officials were entitled to another type of umbrella called *tsumaori-gasa*.

The parasol rather than the umbrella features prominently in Japanese art, especially in famous woodblocks from the 18th and 19th centuries. Generally treated as an item of flirtation, the parasol often half-hides or half-reveals naked or half-robed women walking besides rivers or lakes. Utamaro showed in *Two Beauties under an Umbrella* an amazing multi-coloured example of the parasol, a huge and elaborate artefact despite being obviously made of paper.

Utagawa Hiroshige similarly portrayed women using paper umbrellas in *Evening Snow at Asakusa,* a marvellous work of c.1845. The umbrella, even of the flimsier sort, can protect against snow as well as rain elsewhere. When it snowed heavily in Rome in 2012, many Romans likewise hoisted umbrellas against the descending flakes.

Geisha girls would use decorated sunshades and fans in Tokyo tea-houses as part of their seductive tea ceremonies. Acrobats used simple parasols as part of their acts, teetering under umbrellas on high wires or at the tops of ladders in ways which hugely impressed the French writer Théophile Gautier when he saw them perform. For the Japanese, the parasol was central to their aesthetic view of the world.

Overpage: The ultimate Power Parasol. This massive umbrella or parasol – it would have been equally effective against rain or sun – comes from Ghana in the late 1920s, when it was under British rule. Beneath the main umbrella, various British officials in their starched white uniforms receive local dignitaries. Just visible among them is the Prince of Wales, later Edward VIII, with his distinctive features. Although the main umbrella hardly fits the category of 'mobile home' – it must have taken many strong men to move such a monster – it remains probably the largest umbrella of which photographic records survive. But many African rulers had almost equally huge umbrellas.

Umbrellas are carried by almost everyone in modern Japan, including Shinto
priests, here blessing a local baseball ground and praying for good weather...and
good luck for the home team.

CHAPTER TWO
The Umbrella Goes West

The ancient Greeks and Romans also had parasols and umbrellas but used them very differently from the Assyrians, Persians and Egyptians. With no kings to glorify, they saw them not as power-props but as light-hearted accessories. However, the Greeks did make use of parasols in religious rites.

Women, barred from public life in ancient Greece, took an active part in the rites of goddesses such as Athene, patron deity of Athens. When performing these in the open, women often had parasols. While Greek men loved to exercise naked, getting a good overall tan, Greek women tried to remain fashionably pale-skinned – as all women did until the 1920s, when Coco Chanel revolutionised attitudes to sunbathing.

When Aphrodite, the love goddess, is portrayed on vases, she is often shaded by elegant parasols to protect her snow-white skin. Persephone, goddess of vegetation, also appears on vase paintings under a parasol. This might possibly be an umbrella, for Persephone's symbolic re-emergence from Hades occurred each spring, a rainy season in Greece.

Parasols pop up too in the rites of the wine god Dionysos (Bacchus). Whether in rustic revels in the sticks of Arcadia or in giant processions in cities such as Alexandria, parasols were carried by the Bassarids, Dionysos' raving female followers. In Alexandria a huge statue of Dionysos was shaded by a parasol. However Dionysos, an ambivalent god sexually, was the only Greek god to sport a sunshade. Parasols were normally only used by females, mortal or divine. The poet Anacreon once mocked a man for carrying an ivory-handled parasol 'like a woman'.

In ancient Rome, too, only women used parasols. The poet Juvenal, writing c.AD100, used the term *umbella,* meaning 'little shade', clearly referring to sunshades. In the imperial capital these became luxurious status symbols. According to Pliny, the author killed by the eruption of Vesuvius in AD79, palm leaves were used for early parasol covers and bamboo canes for the frames. Later, covers were made of purple-dyed silks while handles were of ivory studded with gems. Clearly these were luxury items only for sunny days. Yet when Juvenal in another poem recommended taking an *umbella* in case of bad weather, he presumably meant an umbrella.

Earlier the poet Virgil had talked of leather *umbellae*, suggesting something rain-resistant. The technology the Roman parasol/umbrella finally achieved still baffles archaeologists and literary clues remain

The half-naked woman on the left of this Roman mosaic of c.330 from Piazza Armerina, Sicily, is notable for two things: her parasol, twirled in flirtatious dalliance, and her bikini, the first such sighting, one not to recur for 1600 years.

tantalisingly indecisive. Parasols could, however, be fun.

In mosaics of about AD330 in the Roman villa at Piazza Armerina in Sicily, a half-naked woman holding a tiny parasol pirouettes flirtatiously. She is notable for another reason: this is the first recorded sighting of the bikini. (The world would have to wait another 1600 years before the bikini gained wider acceptance.)

With the fall of the Roman Empire, the appeal of the umbrella and parasol declined. They were now used only to symbolise power and dignity. Pope Paul I awarded Pepin, King of the Franks, a bejewelled umbrella in 760 as a reward for protecting the papacy. The *ombrellino* (Italian) or *umbraculum* (Latin) became central to papal regalia. On a mosaic in the church of the Santi Quattro Coronati (Four Crowned Saints) in Rome, Pope Sylvester I (reigned 314-335) receives the imperial insignia, including a large brown-and-white umbrella, from Constantine, the first Christian emperor. A small parasol like a lampshade hovers near the pope's head.

The ceremonial umbrella retained its role at the papal court. A mural in the Palazzo Farnese in Rome shows Pope Eugenius IV (reigned 1431-1447) seated under a flag with the papal insignias of umbrella and crossed keys. The association continues. When

In ancient Greece and Rome parasols were carried only by women, who used them to protect their skin and to flirt.

Pope John Paul II visited Africa in 1985, he was sheltered by a parasol far larger than needed to emphasise his spiritual authority.

Secular rulers deployed super-shades too. In 1177 Pope Alexander III awarded the Doge of Venice the right to a ceremonial umbrella for having arranged a meeting with the Emperor Frederick I. The Doge from then on had an attendant carrying an elaborate umbrella above him until the end of the Venetian Republic in 1797. Canaletto painted several scenes showing the Doge processing under such a parasol.

The Renaissance saw the return of the fun parasol in the Mediterranean world. In 1578 the French writer Henri Estienne mentioned a 'device' that 'certain persons of rank in Spain and Italy carry less to protect themselves against flies than against the sun… [it is] supported on a stick and so made that it takes up little room when folded.' He added that French women would think any Frenchman carrying one effeminate. The philosopher Montaigne noted in 1580 that women in Lucca in Tuscany carried sunshades 'used in Italy since the time of the ancient Romans'.

The English traveller Thomas Coryat, visiting Italy in 1608, also noted Italian umbrellas: 'Many Italians carry other costly items which they commonly call in Italian *umbrellas*, things that minister shadow unto them against the scorching heat of the sun. These are made of leather… and hooped inside with diverse little wooden hoops that extend the umbrella in a pretty large compass.' For Coryat, umbrellas seemed almost as exotic as turbans.

Slowly the sunshade habit spread. It probably first entered France in 1533 with Catherine de' Medici, a Florentine who married King Henri II. Henri's mistress Diane de Poitiers had a famous parasol of silk with an elaborate handle, elegant if heavy. Mary Queen of Scots, who was briefly also queen of France, owned a 'little canopy of crimson satin… with fringes and tassels made of gold and crimson silk… to make a shadow for the queen'.

The Doge of Venice in solemn progress through Venice beneath a massive parasol of state (from a 16th-century print). After the Doge had arranged a meeting between the Pope and the Emperor in 1177, the Pope granted the Doge the right henceforth to a ceremonial umbrella.

A parasol of Henri IV, king of France from 1589 to 1610, was decorated with gold fleur-de-lys, the French royal emblems. His son Louis XIII owned 'five Turkish and German umbrellas for use in the sun' in 1619; by 1637 the royal brolly collection had grown to include eleven taffeta sunshades and three umbrellas of cloth, oiled against the rain and trimmed with gold and silver lace. A grandiose example of this French 'parasol of state' appears in Lebrun's portrait of Pierre Séguier, chancellor of France, entering Paris with Louis XIV in 1660.

Chancellor Pierre Séguier, a minister of Louis XIV, portrayed by Charles Lebrun, making his ceremonial entrance into Paris in 1660. A man of immense vanity, he required *two* power-parasols.

He has *two* ornate parasols to shelter him, born by servants walking beside his horse.

At the new court of Versailles, French women found parasols indispensable for elegant flirtation. In 1678 the philosopher John Locke, on a visit to France, observed that 'Sunshades are small, very light articles, used by ladies here to shield themselves from the sun.'

A major problem with early umbrellas was weight. In 1704 Jean Marius, a Parisian retailer, devised an umbrella with folding ribs and a screwed stick in three sections that could, he claimed, be easily dismantled and weighed only six ounces (140gm). This made it perfect for women to carry but his design did not catch on for some reason. During the 18th century French men began using umbrellas too. In 1760 Horace Walpole noticed that Parisian men 'walk about streets in the rain with umbrellas to avoid putting on hats' and so spoiling their wigs. Little wonder that Diderot included an entry on umbrella-making in his famous *Encyclopédie*.

The Germans followed the French in brollyphilia: in 1734 the *Frankfurter Intelligenzblatt* advertised 'small umbrellas with fringes against the sun and large yellow and brown ones for rainy weather'. Even Frederick the Great of Prussia was painted as a boy under a parasol held by an attendant, although he did not use one later in life as king.

Yet the umbrella was slow to win acceptance across the Channel. When finally the umbrella found a home in the British Isles, it did so solely as a rain shield. Jonathan Swift, in his *A Tale of the Tub* of 1704, referred to 'a large skin of parchment' serving someone as an 'umbrella in rainy weather.' Writing for *The Tatler*, he also mentioned umbrellas of oiled cloth used exclusively by women.

British umbrellas in the early 18th century were still unwieldy objects. The odd large specimen was kept by the front doors of grand houses for footmen to carry over the heads of people hurrying to waiting coaches. If they were too heavy for women to carry easily, any man using one was thought effeminate. It took two exceptional Englishmen – one fictional, one historical – to change such prejudices.

Robinson Crusoe by Daniel Defoe, published in 1719, became the world's first best-seller. The umbrella/parasol plays such a vital part in the desert island saga that the relevant passage deserves quoting in full:

'After this, I spent a great deal of time and pains to make an umbrella; I was, indeed, in great want of one, and had a great mind to make one; I had seen them made in the Brazils, where they are very useful in the great heats there, and I felt the heats every jot as great here, and greater too, being nearer the equinox [equator]; besides, as I was obliged to be much abroad, it was a most useful thing to me, as well

Robinson Crusoe, the hero of Defoe's novel, made himself a parasol/umbrella, judging it an essential item for a desert island castaway. Friday was deeply impressed by such sophistication.

for the rains as the heats. I took a world of pains with it, and was a great while before I could make anything likely to hold: nay, after I had thought I had hit the way, I spoiled two or three before I made one to my mind: but at last I made one that answered indifferently well: the main difficulty I found was to make it let down. I could make it spread, but if it did not let down too, and draw in, it was not portable for me any way but just over my head, which would not do. However, at last, as I said, I made one to answer, and covered it with skins, the hair upwards, so that it cast off the rain like a pent-house, and kept off the sun so effectually, that I could walk out in the hottest of the weather with greater advantage than I could before in the coolest, and when I had no need of it could close it, and carry it under my arm.'

Seldom have the problems and benefits of the umbrella and/or sunshade been so cogently stated. For some time umbrellas were known as Crusoes across Europe.

But to establish the umbrella's street credibility in Britain needed more than a book. It needed Jonas Hanway (1712-86), a merchant who had travelled through Russia and Persia. Influenced by what he had seen on his travels, Hanway on his return to London in 1750 began carrying an umbrella with him whenever rain threatened. At first he was widely mocked, although he used it more to protect his elaborate clothes and wig than himself. The rich, who in their carriages or sedan chairs had no need of umbrellas, sneered at those who did. But, well before his death, Hanway's determined brolly-carrying had made the umbrella an accepted part of a gentleman's getup. (He was eccentric, however. He used to wear flannel underwear and three pairs of wool stockings *at the same time* for his health's sake and attacked the drinking of tea as endangering life and morals.)

The greatest hero in the umbrella's long history is Jonas Hanway. For decades in the 18th century he walked through the streets of London carrying an umbrella, ignoring the multitude's mockery. By the time of his death in 1786, he had converted Londoners to the virtues of brolly-carrying. Fittingly, he has a memorial in Westminster Abbey.

The umbrella habit spread across the Atlantic. As early as 1738 Edward Shippen – a Quaker, so no frivolous follower of fashion – had umbrellas imported into Philadelphia. In June 1768 the *Boston Evening Post* carried an advertisement for 'umbrilloes made and sold by Isaac Greenwood Turner in his shop in Front Street.' These were of various woods, including luxury items of mahogany with ivory ferrules, and were intended for women. In 1772 another Philadelphian merchant imported a crimson silk parasol with an ivory handle from India. This proved too flamboyant for local tastes. One Quaker girl who delighted in a similar parasol was reproved by a Quaker elder with the chilling question: 'Miriam, would thee want that held over thee when thee was a-dying?'

Although *Town and Country Magazine* in Britain snorted that 'philosophers of puppyism [conceitedness] may be met with in every part of the town with umbrellas under their arms', the umbrella began to be accepted in Britain. In 1787 the Royal Society decreed that for members 'if the weather be rainy, an insulated umbrella may be carried in one hand.' That year Thomas Folgham of Cheapside in east London advertised 'a great assortment of his much approved pocket and portable umbrellas, which for lightness, elegance and strength far exceed anything ever imported or manufactured in this kingdom.' Many different types of umbrella were now being produced.

In France, when the Third Estate was locked out of the Assembly on 20 June 1789, they defiantly raised umbrellas against the rain, keeping themselves dry and in fighting form. So the umbrella had a small role in the French Revolution.

Attitudes to brollies can be revealing. On the left a Regency dandy strolls proudly, his umbrella thrust out before him; in the centre a man of the middle class holds a bulky but decent brolly as he walks with his family; on the right a wretch, unlucky at love or at cards or at both, slouches away, his tatty umbrella dragging on the ground.

CHAPTER THREE

The Classic Umbrella Arrives

As the 18th century turned into the 19th, there came a revolution in men's clothing, one associated with Beau Brummell, the 'first dandy'. Out went the old lace, silks, jewellery and wigs. In came a more sober look, dependent for effect on the cut of a coat in relatively muted colours, and on pristine white linen. The change generally suited the umbrella, an item now used by all classes and both sexes, people who walked rather than rode. In 1810 the *Universal Magazine* reported in disgust that the umbrella 'is now made of such cheap material that it is in the hands of every class'.

The material for the better type of umbrella was oiled silk: waterproof, flexible but heavy. This must have been the sort of umbrella purchased in Bath by Captain Wentworth in Jane Austen's *Persuasion* (1818). Cheaper brollies were made of linen or cottons. Called *gamps*, these were very bulky and not always rain-repellent. 'Gamp' comes from Mrs Gamp, a disreputable old nurse in Dickens' *Martin Chuzzlewit* (1844). Her grubby patched gamp proves unmanageable inside a coach: 'it several times thrust out its battered brass nozzle from improper crevices and chinks to the great terror of other passengers.'

Gamps were inelegant, even ludicrous. A joke made about Louis-Philippe, the 'bourgeois' king of France, was that he always carried a gamp when out walking in his attempt to appear a man of the people. (The attempt failed: Louis-Philippe was toppled by revolution in 1848.) As the century grew more sombre in its clothes and more earnest in its habits, black umbrellas became a central part of a sober citizen's outfit, along with black top hat and coat. Impressionist artists –

Manet, Pissarro, Monet, Gustave Caillebotte – delighted in painting umbrellas on the Paris boulevards newly built by Haussmann. Black and grey are the dominant colours of these rain-splashed scenes, suiting a utilitarian age.

The umbrella's potential for flirtation can hardly be overstated. In this fashion-plate of 1826, a young woman gazes out alluringly from the shade of her parasol.

In the early 19th century, however, by no means all umbrellas were utilitarian. George IV, an extravagantly dandified monarch, had a huge umbrella of pink silk with a striped border. Brummell, when in penurious exile in France, had an ivory-handled one decorated with a satirical portrait of George, with whom he had by then fallen out.

Dandies differed over umbrellas. Many found walking-sticks far more elegant. Honoré de Balzac, the first man to write on dandyism – in *Traité de la vie élégante* (Treatise on Elegant Living, 1830) – damned the umbrella as 'a bastard born of the walking stick and the cabriolet.' Some years later, however, the comte d'Orsay, a flamboyant dandy, declared that if he could not have a decent carriage, he would be content with a fine umbrella. Despite d'Orsay's own bravura, the male umbrella gradually became a uniform black. Only handles, variously made of ivory, teak, mahogany, cane or rattan, allowed for any real individuality. For women, however, parasols of ingenious delicacy proliferated in many colours.

This was a fashion boosted in London by the young Queen Victoria who habitually carried one when riding in an open carriage. W. & J. Sangsters of Regent Street, London, became the smartest suppliers of parasols, producing new designs every year. In 1843 they created the Pekin in striped materials; in 1844 came La Sylphide. This had a button near the handle to release a spring making it collapsible with only one hand. It came 'in every variety of shape and material'. A deluxe model was the Claremont, which weighed only half as much as an ordinary silk parasol but cost three times as much (5s 6d, or 27p). Handles were often carved into fantastic shapes: lions, dragons, horses or greyhounds.

In 1851 the Great Exhibition in London showcased the umbrellas and parasols now being made in Britain and France. Sangsters displayed the La Sylphide parasol along with models trimmed with feathers, satin and lace and won a prize for their 'silk parasols and umbrellas of excellent quality and for their application of alpaca cloth to the coverings of Parasols and Umbrellas.' Alpaca wool, as tough and water-resistant as oiled silk but cheaper and lighter, swiftly became a common umbrella covering. In 1854 the Sangsters sold 45,000 such alpaca umbrellas. By 1871 William Sangster claimed that his firm had sold four million. That year he published his *Umbrellas and their History,* a slim history of umbrellas, the first proper one in English. Only at the end does he mention his own products.

The introduction around the year 1840 of steel ribs in place of whalebone or cane made umbrellas and parasols cheaper, lighter and more durable, for cane quickly wore out and whalebone tended to crack. Samuel Fox in 1852 developed the 'Paragon Umbrella' with a

The Beach at Trouville by Claude Monet. In 1870 Monet painted five such beach scenes, all celebrations of the parasol. The women on the left carefully protecting herself from the sun's rays is his wife Camille.

U-section rib and stretcher, so producing what was in effect the first modern umbrella. His design enabled ribs to come far closer to the stick, making (furled) umbrellas much slimmer.

Among other parasol-makers were Henry Holland of Birmingham whose patent umbrella weighed just 9oz (250gm); William Slark of the Burlington Arcade, London, who created a lady's parasol-whip; Wilson and Matheson of Glasgow who produced an umbrella that folded into a walking-stick; and I. A. Boss of London who displayed the 'Royal Victoria Parasol', with gilded hexagonal stick and gold handle set with diamonds and decorated with the Order of the Garter. This was duly presented to the Queen herself.

Some firms still thriving today were already making their mark. In 1862 James Smith & Co were selling five lengths of Paragon

The Bayswater Omnibus by G. W. Joy, 1895, tellingly contrasts the colourful parasol held by the young woman in the centre, and the sombre umbrella held by the man sitting next to her, which he keeps tight-furled.

umbrellas, from 21½ inches to 27½ inches, with silk-covered versions costing up to 21 shillings (£1.05), while alpaca-covered Paragons cost only 9 shillings (45p). Brigg & Son began making their classic Thomas Brigg umbrellas in 1836. Now part of Swaine Adeney Brigg & Co, they have been doing so ever since.

From the end of the 19th century one picture sums up the contrast of parasol and umbrella. *The Bayswater Omnibus* by G. W. Joy of 1895 depicts side by side a parasol, held by the attractive young woman in the centre, and an umbrella, held by the older man sitting next to her. Her parasol is colourful, matching the flowers she is holding. It is nearly half-open as if she might shortly use it as an umbrella, for the day outside looks damply autumnal. In contrast, the umbrella of the man, who is soberly well dressed, has a classic black form. It is tight-furled and probably will never be opened except in extremely heavy rain.

CHAPTER FOUR

The Umbrella at War

Brollyphilia, the passion for umbrellas, attained fresh heights in 19th-century armies. It proved especially strong among British officers, a notoriously dandified lot, who carried umbrellas even onto the battlefield.

In December 1813, when the British were besieging Bayonne in western France – a city with a rainfall higher even than Glasgow's – officers in the Grenadier Guards raised their umbrellas against the Atlantic storms. The Duke of Wellington, their general, was not amused. He sent a message forbidding his officers 'the use of umbrellas during the enemy's firing... I will not allow gentlemen's sons to make themselves ridiculous in the eyes of the army,' he declared. 'Officers may, when on [guard] duty at St James's in London, carry umbrellas but in the field it is not only ridiculous but unmilitary.'

Wellington's strictures had little effect. The following year several British officers entered Paris in triumph *holding green silk parasols*. The Duke – who was himself something of a dandy in an austere, taciturn way – had an umbrella of oiled cloth which also was a swordstick. At that time the umbrella, precisely because it was still so bulky, could easily conceal a sword in its handle. Besides its obvious functions, the umbrella swordstick could be also used in matters of courtesy. In 1813 a captured officer of the French 15th Hussars offered General Alten, commanding the British Light Division, his umbrella swordstick against the rain.

At the battle of Waterloo in 1815 Marshall Soult, a French commander, was amazed by the flagrant brollyphilia of British officers.

He dubbed them 'les efféminés avec leurs parapluies' (effeminates with their umbrellas). 'It was raining and the English officers on horseback each held an umbrella in their hand,' he recalled. 'This seemed to me very ridiculous. But suddenly the English closed their umbrellas, hung them upon their saddles and threw themselves upon our Chasseurs.' Fighting spirit maintained by having kept their uniforms immaculate, the British won the day.

The French themselves, despite Soult's disdain, had already found military uses for the umbrella. Before the battle of Austerlitz on 1st December 1805 the emperor Napoleon spent the night going round his troops' bivouacs. He was greeted by cheers and loud cries of 'Vive l'empereur!' – it was exactly one year since he had crowned himself emperor. He then retired to a desk in the open for a last-minute consultation with his generals. Over the assembled generals and his imperial majesty a tall officer of the *Garde Impériale* stood holding a giant umbrella. Shielded from the elements, Napoleon planned the most brilliant victory of his career.

Earlier, during the short-lived Peace of Amiens (1802-03), British visitors to Paris had been amused to see soldiers of the French National Guard doing their drill during showers with a musket in one hand and an umbrella in the other – a feat that even the most clothes-conscious of British soldiers did not attempt.

Years later Lord Raglan, who had been one of Wellington's officers in the Napoleonic wars, took a large umbrella with him when he set off for his disastrous command in the Crimean War. What happened to Raglan's umbrella after the unhappy commander-in-chief died in the Crimea in 1855 is unknown but the umbrella gradually lost much of its appeal in military circles. By the end of the 19th century the field uniforms of the British army had dulled down to khaki, a colour so drab that fewer and fewer soldiers felt any need to protect their uniforms.

Many years earlier the umbrella had played a less glorious part in the murder of Giuseppe Prina. He was the finance minister of the Kingdom of Italy, at that time a client state of Napoleon Bonaparte. Appointed in 1805, Prina had imposed such severe taxes to meet Napoleon's demands that he became the most hated man in Italy. When Napoleon's empire collapsed in April 1814, a riot erupted called the 'Battle of the Umbrellas'. An angry mob broke into the Senate House and dragged Prina out. The unhappy minister was clubbed to death with umbrellas in front of Milan cathedral.

Perhaps aware of this precedent, and growing nervous after an assassination attempt, Queen Victoria experimented with an umbrella lined with chain mail. Unsurprisingly, she found it intolerably heavy and abandoned it. Another group of Victorians, however, combined armour and umbrellas in a remarkable way.

Archibald Montgomerie, 13th Earl of Eglinton, was an unusually dreamy romantic even for the 19th century. Disgusted by the prosaic

The so-called 'Battle of the Umbrellas' of April 1814 saw Giuseppe Prina, the finance minister for the Kingdom of Italy, clubbed to death with umbrellas outside Milan Cathedral. Seldom has the brolly been used so brutally.

nature of the Whig government – which had tried to 'modernise' Queen Victoria's coronation in 1838 by abolishing the traditional banquet – Eglinton determined to recreate the splendours of a medieval joust at his castle in Ayrshire. Ayrshire is a famously beautiful part of Scotland; it is also a very wet one. The local saying goes that if you can see the mountains in the morning, it will rain by midday; if you cannot see them, it is raining already. Ignoring this ancestral wisdom, Eglinton set out to resuscitate the custom of jousting in full armour, something last attempted in Britain before 1640.

The project inspired gallant young aristocrats across Europe, with over 100 applying to take part. The ever-generous Eglinton also sent out countless invitations, expecting about 4,000 spectators. In the event, about 100,000 turned up, causing logistical chaos. Worse, it began to rain very heavily on the morning of the joust, causing most of the marquees and tents to leak and making the grounds a marsh.

Skidding in the mud, their armour growing rustier by the minute, the 'knights' attempted to joust. They generally had little success. They had not trained themselves and their horses for such trials for many years, as medieval knights used to, and their horses shied away from the central barrier, making any contact impossible. Meanwhile, spectators got wetter and wetter, despite a sea of raised umbrellas.

One pair of knights, however, apparently kept on jousting *under umbrellas*. Or so it was reported by witnesses. Only a quick sketch that became a cartoon recorded the incident, for the camera had not yet been invented. Convincing proof that the umbrella can play a part in medieval (mock) warfare.

Six years later *Punch* magazine satirically suggested that umbrellas should be fixed to soldiers' guns. It published a cartoon showing two columns charging each other, each shielded from the rain by umbrellas. Beneath ran the verse:

March to the battle-field
We fear not horrida bella
Dastard is the slave who'd yield
Wave high the stout umbrella.

Amid the horrors of 20th-century warfare the umbrella might have seemed to have no role, but it cropped up in odd places. In the First World War, British soldiers captured at Kut in Iraq by the Turks in 1916 bought umbrellas to use as sunshades during their long march into captivity. In the same war, British officers fighting in northern France used umbrellas when map-reading or writing messages. At the Battle of Armentières in 1914 so many officers raised their umbrellas 'that the front line began to look like a pallid imitation of a wet day at Ascot.' Most brollies were used while waiting in the trenches but Captain Raymond Green of the 9th Lancers carried his into action during the first Battle of Messines in 1914.

So, more gloriously, did Major Allison Digby Tatham-Warter 30 years

A cartoon from *Punch* magazine in 1845 mocks the importance of umbrellas to dandified soldiers, even on the field of battle.

later. While the Second World War was not an umbrella-friendly conflict – mechanised fighting moved too fast for proper brolly deployment – at one famous battle the umbrella came into its own. In September 1944 the Allies attempted to seize the bridges over the Rhine at Arnhem. British parachutists led the assault but were cut off and left facing far superior German armoured forces. Their situation was soon desperate but one British officer decided not to take it too seriously.

Digby Tatham-Warter was already noted for his courage and sang froid, a man who would 'have been a great cavalry commander on the

A Brolly Too Far. In September 1944 the Allied attempt to seize the Rhine bridges at Arnhem led to British paratroops being cut off by German armoured forces. Undaunted, Major Digby Tatham-Warter strolled around under enemy fire carrying an umbrella for protection – against the odd spot of rain. At one point he led a charge wearing a bowler hat and waving his umbrella. His action was recreated in the 1967 film, *A Bridge Too Far*.

King's side in the war with the Roundheads' according to his colonel. He had trained his troops to use bugles to communicate, foreseeing that their radios might not work properly. The trumpets proved invaluable. But even better for keeping up fighting spirits was the major's style. He strolled around under heavy enemy fire carrying an umbrella for protection – against the odd spot of rain, that is. At one point he led a bayonet charge wearing an old bowler hat while waving his umbrella. He also disabled a German armoured car by poking his brolly into its observation slit and blinding the driver.

In the shade of their own parasol, Blackhorse Troopers, America's crack armoured troops, check map coordinates from the deck of their M48A1 Patton Tank a few miles east of the Cambodian border in March, 1971.

Tatham-Warter later said that he 'carried the umbrella more for identification purposes than for anything else because I was always forgetting the password and it would be quite obvious to anyone that the bloody fool carrying the umbrella could only be an Englishman.' If this underestimates the umbrella's global appeal, brollies were certainly never sported by his SS opponents.

In the Vietnam War, that even more gruelling conflict, a US tank was photographed in the battlefield. Above its turret is hoisted a flamboyant parasol. While not standard equipment, the parasol gave its crew both useful shade and an élan too often lacking in modern warfare.

Well into the 1960s off-duty officers of the Brigade of Guards in London had to adhere to a strict dress-code: bowler hat, dark suit, highly polished shoes and, of course, a furled brolly (and when so dressed travelling on any mode of public transport and even carrying a parcel was frowned upon). Today off-duty officers' dress codes are in line with the rest of the population. On occasion they continue to sport immaculately furled umbrellas and bowler hats, come rain or

Guards officers off-duty with their (then) mandatory brollies and bowlers, c.1960. Their high sartorial standards have since sadly declined.

shine, but only when attending certain military events in civilian clothes.

In March 2011 Nicolas Sarkozy, a president of France who knew that he had become unprecedentedly unpopular, ordered a special Kevlar-coated umbrella for use by his bodyguards. Costing £10,000, it could have been opened to cover the diminutive figure of the president – only 5ft 5 inches tall – if danger threatened. The umbrella was never called into action, but it was so strong that the presidential bodyguards were able to smash tables with it.

Perhaps the most infamous use of the umbrella in war – the Cold War, that is – was the assassination of the Bulgarian defector Georgi Markov. Markov had been a novelist and playwright in his native Bulgaria until 1969, when he had fled to Britain for political asylum. He then worked for the BBC World Service and Radio Free Europe. In broadcasts to Bulgaria he made repeated withering attacks on Bulgaria's communist government. His personal ridicule of the party leader Todor Zhivkov made him a special enemy of the regime. Sentenced to six years in prison in absentia, Markov continued to make his broadcasts, although he knew he was risking his life. Bulgarian spies, aided by the KGB, reputedly made two failed attempts on his life, first in Munich and then in Sardinia. They finally had success at their third attempt in London – with the help of a poisoned umbrella.

On the morning of September 7th 1978, Markov was waiting in a bus queue by Waterloo Bridge in London with other commuters when he felt a sudden sharp pain. He had been pricked in the leg by an umbrella. This belonged to a man who apologised for his 'clumsiness' in a foreign accent before hastily making off in a taxi. On arrival at work, Markov noticed a small painful red bump on his calf. That evening he developed a fever and he died four days later. The umbrella had contained in its shaft a disguised pellet gun firing the pellet which had killed him.

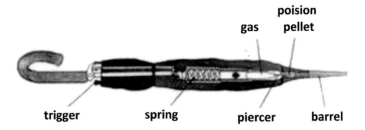

poision
gas pellet
trigger spring piercer barrel

A diagram of the poison-tipped umbrella used to assassinate the dissident Bulgarian writer Georgi Markov in London in 1978 in case of the Poisonous Umbrella. The murderer of Markov has still not been unearthed.

A post mortem examination revealed a platinum pellet embedded in his flesh. It contained 0.2gm of the deadly poison Ricin, coated with a plastic designed to melt at 37 degrees C (98.4 F), blood temperature. Subsequently several KGB defectors have confirmed that the KGB, the Soviet Union's secret service, was behind the assassination. Although the coroner's court at the time determined that Markov had been 'unlawfully killed', no one has ever been charged with his murder.

The story has a James Bond touch to it, although it lacks the witty inventiveness of special weapons in the best Bond films.

CHAPTER FIVE

The Umbrella in Politics

By the mid-19th century the link between the umbrella and power had broken. The power parasol was likewise dead. However, the umbrella, now an emblem of middle-class respectability, was carried by many democratic politicians anxious to win votes. It became associated with some famous British prime ministers.

The most flamboyant was Benjamin Disraeli. A noted dandy, social mountaineer and romantic writer, he was the first – and last – British novelist to become prime minister. Disraeli in his later years had to tone down his style to advance in politics, although by the 1850s overt dandyism was out of fashion in Britain anyway. An aspect of his new sobriety was his umbrella. This was an unspectacular plain black brolly, almost resembling a gamp in its shabbiness.

Disraeli's great rival William Gladstone, the austere Liberal leader who also became prime minister many times, was famous for his umbrellas. These baggy items were indisputably gamps. Gamps accompanied Gladstone on the heroic election campaigns that took him around Britain when he gave long speeches to rapt crowds in the open air, come rain or shine. Not everyone was impressed. In a *Punch* cartoon from 1885 Gladstone is shown sadly holding a battered old brolly and saying, 'My umbrella needs recovering.' Stepping out from a shop Joseph Chamberlain, then a rising Liberal politician, responds: 'Step inside, sir. Recover it while you wait!' The Victorians often had their umbrellas recovered but *Punch* was commenting acidly on Gladstone's tattered old *policies*. The Grand Old Man of British politics, by then 77 years old, was doggedly trying to get his first Irish Home Rule Bill passed.

Walking briskly down Whitehall in 1914, Lloyd George and Winston Churchill, both members of the Liberal government, reveal different attitudes towards the umbrella. Lloyd George carries one but keeps it furled, while Churchill, undaunted by the threat of showers, eschews one completely. He still, however, carries a walking-stick.

A photograph of somewhat later, probably around 1914, shows two men walking along Whitehall in London. One is Lloyd George, then Chancellor of the Exchequer. He is carrying an umbrella but has not unfurled it despite the risk of drizzle – many Britons, both at the time and later, *never* unfurled their umbrellas. Beside him hurries the young Winston Churchill, another minister in the Liberal government of the day. Churchill is carrying a walking-stick not an umbrella, as if rain held no terrors for the future war-leader, or perhaps because an umbrella's air-resistance would have slowed down his always rapid pace.

The most notorious appearance of the brolly in politics was at the Munich Conference in 1938. Neville Chamberlain, born in 1869, was only five years older than Churchill but he belonged to an earlier, less frenetic generation. In particular, he always travelled with his

Neville Chamberlain with the umbrella he took to Munich in 1938, perhaps the brolly's most infamous hour. For Chamberlain, his umbrella signified honesty and decency – not qualities appreciated by Hitler.

umbrella, for it suggested British self-assurance, honesty and politeness. When he set out to meet Hitler at Munich in 1938, he took his neatly furled brolly with him on the aircraft. (This was Chamberlain's very first flight.)

Hitler, like most dictators, had no time for umbrellas. Umbrellas do not go with jackboots and steel helmets. 'If that silly old man comes interfering here again with his umbrella, I'll kick him downstairs and jump on him,' he reportedly said after Chamberlain had left. But others across Europe were more impressed, both by the treaty – very few people in Europe wanted war in 1938 – and by Chamberlain's umbrella. Some Italians, delighted by this *stile inglese* (English style), even wrote to No 10 Downing Street asking for the name of the premier's umbrella-maker. They received a frosty refusal to divulge the secret behind Chamberlain's (seeming) success. Yet for a while his type of furled black brolly was known across southern Europe as a 'chamberlain.'

CHAPTER SIX

The Parasol as Erotic Alchemy

The connection of parasols and love goes back at least 2,000 years to Rome. The poet Ovid in his *Ars Amatoria* (Art of Love) advised young men on how to impress their girl friends:

> *'You yourself must hold her parasol above her*
> *And with it clear her way ahead through the crowds'*

This was a radical idea in imperial Rome, where only slaves carried parasols for their mistresses. But Ovid could point to the example of Hercules, the mythical super-hero who had briefly served Queen Omphale as a slave, carrying 'a golden parasol to block off the fierce sun.' Ovid was finally banished by the emperor Augustus for such improper suggestions and the parasol's erotic potential was finally forgotten with the fall of Rome.

In the 17th and 18th centuries the seductive parasol reappeared at the court of Versailles. The nobles of France, in theory assembled to boost royal power, had plenty of time for flirtation and seduction in style. Madame de Pompadour, Louis XV's most famous mistress, had a special parasol made for her of blue silk with Chinese mica ornaments. This style proved so popular that it was revived many times during the 18th and 19th centuries. In the paintings of rococo artists such as Boucher, Delord and Fragonard, parasols shelter the heads of most women who are even half-dressed. The French Revolution in 1789 hardly dimmed the parasol's erotic allure, by now appreciated far beyond the ranks of the old aristocracy.

A card of c.1912 shows a chap wooing a girl partly because of the allure of her parasol, which so subtly matches his umbrella. Her friends, sporting sunshades that are clearly inadequate, can only look on.

René-Marie Cazal was parasol-maker by appointment to Louis-Philippe's dowdy queen and subsequently to Napoleon III's beautiful empress Eugénie. In 1851 he wrote a book, *Essai historique, anecdotique sur le parapluie, l'ombrelle et la canne et sur leur fabrication* (Historical and Anecdotal Essay on the Umbrella, Parasol and Walking-Stick and their Fabrication). In it he praised the wonders of Parisian parasols, especially his own.

'The parasol, like a rosy vapour, attenuates and softens a woman's features, it restores her faded colouring, sheltering her face with diaphanous reflections... Under its rosy or azure dome, passion is born, broods or blossoms. From a distance the sunshade beckons passers-by; nearby it delights the eyes of the curious... How many sweet smiles have played under its Corolla! How many charming signs of the head, how many intoxicating and magic looks? How many emotions and dramas has it hidden under its cloud of silk?'

Cloud of silk... the essence of the parasol's appeal.

The '*Néreides*' – the nicknames of four almost identical sisters – bedazzled Belle Epoque France just before the First World War. As can be seen from the illustration, parasols played a major part in their appeal. While changes in fashion in the 1920s meant that most women now wanted to look tanned, not white, the parasol remained popular even in the south of France. This is evident from one of the century's most famous photographs: that taken by Robert Capa in 1948.

Françoise Gilot was Picasso's most intelligent, most determined and most indomitable mistress. The artist, alpha male as much as genius, had met her during the Second World War when she was 21 and he 61. Their relationship lasted ten years and they had two children, Claude and Paloma. Unlike most other women in Picasso's life, Françoise Gilot had a life of her own before, during and after her relationship with Picasso. A graduate of both the Sorbonne and Cambridge,

Even on pin-up posters the parasol pops up. *I've been Spotted!* by Gil Elvgren, king of such art, c.1949, shows that a model's parasol is as much part of her sex-appeal as her stocking tops.

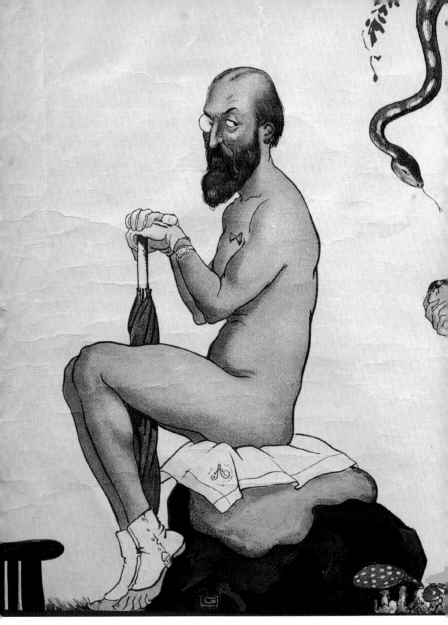

Even in the Garden of Eden the umbrella and parasol can be found. This detail –
from a remarkable mural in the Lansdowne Club, London made by an unknown
French artist in the early 20th century – shows Adam and Eve in a new light. The
dandified Adam, with his spats, monocle, wristwatch and gloves, an embroidered

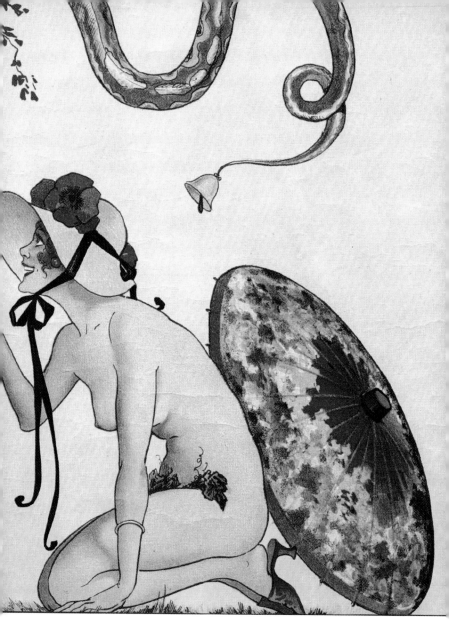

handkerchief protecting his fastidious buttocks, has his brolly carefully furled. Eve, however, with her straw hat, lipstick and red high-heeled mules, has deployed her polychromatic parasol as she tries to seduce Adam into the joys of forbidden fruit. The weather in Eden presumably included sudden light showers.

Françoise Gilot sheltered by a parasol carried by Picasso in Robert Capa's famous 1948 photograph. Gilot was the artist's most intelligent and forceful mistress, so there was a pointed irony in having Picasso, that ultra-macho painter, portrayed carrying her parasol. This was a role, as he well knew, reserved for servants or slaves in the past.

she was an artist and author as well as mistress and muse. After she left Picasso – escaping the painter's orbit almost unscathed – she married Jonas Salk, inventor of the polio vaccine.

So it is fitting that in Robert Capa's 1948 photograph of the painter and his muse on the beach it is Picasso who is the parasol-bearer, a role so often associated in legend with slaves or servants. Picasso, who knew his Greek myths, may have been echoing Hercules, if ironically – there is certainly nothing slave-like in his attitude. But Françoise walks like the queen she certainly was.

Adolf Hitler was a dictator so exclusively obsessed with power that he is thought seldom if ever to have had sex with anyone. He did, however, have a long-standing mistress, Eva Braun. A blonde of such reputed dumbness that Albert Speer said she 'would prove a great disappointment to historians', Eva was interested in fashion, amateur photography, sport – she swam in a lake near Berchtesgaden, Hitler's Alpine retreat – and cinema. She was also, it appears, interested in posing nude for the camera – nude, that is, except for a parasol/umbrella. Hitler would probably not have been amused if he had known. Almost certainly he did not. If Eva Braun had been attempting to arouse his interest, diverting it from world conquest to her own person, she failed. But the photograph shows that, even in the heart of darkness, a parasol could raise its seductive head for a moment.

If only the Führer had known about it... Eva Braun, Hitler's mistress posing practically naked apart from a colourful parasol, failed to deflect the dictator from his murderous ambitions. But then Hitler, a notorious brollyphobe and teetotaller, probably did not know of Eva's parasol pictures.

CHAPTER SEVEN

The Brolly on Stage and Screen

Charlie Chaplin made a decrepit brolly – a gamp, really – part of his classic 'tramp' image in his early films, but this was an undignified stage role for such an elegant item. Only later did the umbrella and parasol find the star roles on stage and screen that they deserved. Oddly, three of the most famous umbrella/parasol films, all of them superb musicals, appeared in the same year: 1964. As it was not a year noted for its rainfall, the triple premieres indicate that humankind's earliest mobile home was still high in fashion in the 1960s. Only one of the films is actually set in that dizzy decade, however. The other two look back to the gilded age before 1914.

The Umbrellas of Cherbourg (Les Parapluies de Cherbourg), the sole contemporary work, stars Catherine Deneuve as Geneviève and Nino Castelnuovo as Guy, with music by Michel Legrand. Geneviève, who works in her mother's umbrella boutique in Cherbourg, falls in love with Guy, a handsome young car mechanic. Under their umbrellas in steady rain, they declare their love in a series of touching duets. Love does not run smoothly, however, for she

In *Les Parapluies de Cherbourg* (The Umbrellas of Cherbourg), the famed French musical of 1964, the umbrella plays a pivotal role. Without it, the young lovers would have been drowned before their first kiss.

becomes pregnant and he is called up to fight in Algeria for two years. Feeling neglected when Guy fails to write, Geneviève is persuaded to marry an older and richer man, although she does not love him. Years later the lovers – Geneviève elegant, wealthy and disillusioned, Guy reasonably content running a garage – meet very briefly again, Guy seeing his son for the first and only time. Meanwhile, it rains.

Unusually, there is no spoken dialogue nor are there any choruses, only a series of recitatives. This makes it a peculiarly French sort of musical. There have been several stage versions of the story, most recently in London, but none wholly captures the gentle melancholy and rained-on lyricism of the film, where umbrellas form a central part of the action. These umbrellas are mostly utilitarian, understandably in view of the weather.

Mary Poppins is utterly different, in part because it is a children's

The umbrella's record in aviation has been unimpressive in life. In art, however, it has often given uplift, as revealed by Mary Poppins' effortless flights over Edwardian London. The musical of 1964 starred Julie Andrews as the umbrella-propelled governess.

film of course. Set in London in 1910 – or Disney's version of the city – it stars Julie Andrews as the flying governess Mary Poppins, 'practically perfect in every way'. She makes her first appearance floating down from the sky with an umbrella. Subsequent umbrella take-offs and balloon-like voyages over London's roofs are among the film's most memorable scenes. (So are Dick Van Dyck's attempts to speak Cockney as Bert, the dancing Jack of All Trades).

Mary Poppins' magical spell is *supercalifragilisticexpialidocious*, uttered whenever things are going badly. At the end, as the wind changes, Mary takes off again with her umbrella. A myriad Mary Poppinses with aero-umbrellas returned to spiral over the London Olympics in 2012, bringing memories of a more elegant era.

In *My Fair Lady* the parasol at last gained recognition on film as a superb instrument of flirtation. This was shown by its appearance – in the hands of Audrey Hepburn – on the original film poster. Audrey Hepburn plays Eliza Doolittle, a Cockney flower-seller dragged out of the gutters of Edwardian London by Professor Higgins (Rex Harrison in one of his finest roles). Higgins, an irascible egocentric bachelor and elocution specialist, bets that he can turn Eliza into a lady of the most refined sort merely by working on her accent. (This was in the days when a cut glass voice was *de rigueur* in English high society). He succeeds, at the expense of poor Eliza's nerves.

At Ascot, that glamorous race meeting, Eliza's elegant yet seductive deployment of a parasol – a skill she cannot have acquired from her rebarbative tutor – adds more to her appeal than her careful vowels. Young Freddie, watching more than listening, is bewitched and falls in love. (All the other women present carry similar parasols, however, for they were thought essential to protect milk-white complexions. Cecil Beaton's famous costume designs if anything underrate the parasol's prominence in the Belle Epoque. As photographs show, women then glided in a foam of white lace as

The umbrella had its finest hour on stage and screen in *My Fair Lady*. The 1964 film starred Audrey Hepburn, raised from the gutter by elocution lessons and by her elegant deployment of her parasol to captivate London high society.

stately and elegant as ocean liners around Henley, Ascot, Goodwood, Baden-Baden, Longchamp and other fashionable meetings.)

These three essentially European films were preceded by an all-American movie, one of the wittiest musicals ever made: *Singin' in the Rain*. The film, starring Gene Kelly as Don Lockwood, a dazzlingly handsome actor who has played so far only in silent movies, and Debbie Reynolds as Kathy Seldon, an aspiring actress, appeared in 1952 but is set in the late 1920s. *Singin' in the Rain* combines vaudeville, musical and satire, digging none too gently into Hollywood pretensions beneath its bonhomie. The climax of the film, with its plot-within-a-plot as talkies replace silent movies, is Gene Kelly's superb song-and-dance *Singin' in the Rain*. Although Kelly generously hands over his umbrella to another soaked pedestrian just before the climax, the umbrella is vital to his performance. Its importance is underlined by the way Kelly with Debbie Reynolds and Donald O' Connor are all shown on the original poster, dancing, wearing raincoats and *carrying umbrellas*.

The wittiest brolly-movie ever made, *Singin' in the Rain* reaches it climax in the scene where Gene Kelly declares his love of Debbie Reynolds in exuberant song-and-dance. Note that he keeps his umbrella closed, despite the downpour.

The umbrella was central to the career of secret agent John Steed, played with understated flair by Patrick Macnee in the 1960s television series *The Avengers*. Throughout Steed looks impeccably elegant with bowler hat, well-cut suits and furled umbrella, the last from the august English firm of Fox. While his female colleagues – notably Diana Rigg as Mrs Peel – at times use guns, Steed never does. Instead he relies on his umbrella to help overthrow the ungodly. Macnee in fact had an aversion to guns, which he had used in real combat in the Second World War. (The whole series is astonishingly non-violent by today's blood-sated standards, however.) The title for the German-dubbed version *Mit Schirm, Charme und Melone*, With Umbrella, Charm and Bowler Hat, encapsulates its ever-green appeal.

In *The New Avengers,* which ran from 1976 to 1977, Macnee reappeared. This time he was flanked by Joanna Lumley as the glamorous agent Purdey, who at times also sported an umbrella and bowler hat. The problems besetting British intelligence services in recent decades may be linked to their agents' neglect of the vital brolly and bowler. (But see page 54 for the poisonous umbrella.)

The greatest cartoon series in the world has among its leading characters a man who is *never* parted from his umbrella: Professor Calculus, Tintin's absent-minded but benevolent super-boffin. The professor is no dandy, for all his Edwardian style, but his umbrella goes with him through thick and thin. The reason for this finally emerges in *The Calculus Affair*. In this supeb espionage book it is revealed that Calculus sometimes hides important secrets – for a sonic weapon, for example – in his brolly's handle. The joy with which Calculus hugs his rediscovered umbrella is one of the high moments of 20th-century graphic art. (The bowler-hatted Thompson twins, those master-detectives, are also inseparable from their umbrellas, although this does not always lead them to the guilty party).

Joanna Lumley as Purdy, co-starring con brio in *The New Avengers* with Patrick Macnee. Note her brolly and bowler, both as essential to a successful secret agent as a revolver.

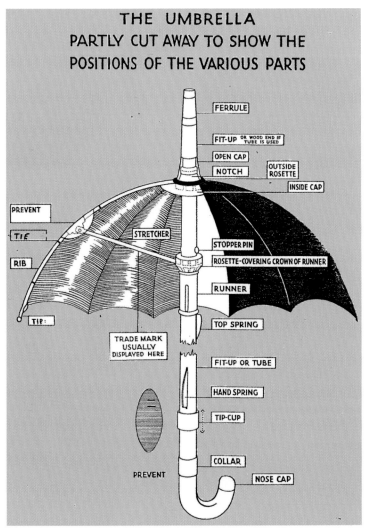

THE UMBRELLA
PARTLY CUT AWAY TO SHOW THE
POSITIONS OF THE VARIOUS PARTS

FERRULE

FIT-UP OR WOOD END IF TUBE IS USED

OPEN CAP

NOTCH

OUTSIDE ROSETTE

INSIDE CAP

PREVENT

TIE

STRETCHER

STOPPER PIN

ROSETTE-COVERING CROWN OF RUNNER

RIB

RUNNER

TIP:

TOP SPRING

TRADE MARK USUALLY DISPLAYED HERE

FIT-UP OR TUBE

HAND SPRING

TIP-CUP

COLLAR

PREVENT

NOSE CAP

The anatomy of the classic umbrella has changed little over the years. Its shape is almost as archetypal as the wheel's.

CHAPTER EIGHT

The Anatomy of the Umbrella

The basic structure or shape of the umbrella, like that of the wheel, has changed little over the millennia. Before dropping in on your local umbrella merchant, however, it can be useful for a true brollyphile to know the technical terms. Such knowledge will impress fellow umbrella-carriers too.

Canopy A canopy, the crown of the umbrella, is made of fabric and deflects the rain or, in the case of the parasol, the sun. It is therefore the most important part. Today almost all umbrella fabrics are of nylon or similar synthetics, which have proved tougher and more flexible than natural fibres. Parasol fabrics are still at times made of cotton. Although most urban umbrellas today have plain black canopies, in the past they have often been remarkably colourful, as many parasols still are.

Ferrule/Finial Essentially ornamental, the ferrule (also called the finial) is the sharp end found at the very top of the umbrella, above the canopy. If the umbrella is carried carelessly, the ferrule may prod those nearby. In the swordstick umbrella, it conceals the weapon's tip, poisoned or otherwise.

Ribs The ribs give an umbrella its essential structure and shape, but they are notoriously vulnerable to sudden gusts of winds. Outer ribs support the canopy while inner ribs (often called stretchers) link the outer ribs with the umbrella pole.

Runner The runner slides up and down the pole while connected to the ribs/stretchers, and is responsible for the opening and closing of the canopy.

Springs Many types of umbrella contain a top spring to hold the runner up when the canopy is open and a bottom spring to hold the runner down when the canopy is closed. In telescopic or collapsible umbrellas, a single ball spring in the centre can extend the pole length. This single spring is one of many reasons why telescopic umbrellas seldom last long.

Stick A stick, also called pole, is the metal or wooden shaft running between the umbrella's handle at the bottom and the canopy at the top. It can also be made of plastic, bamboo or, for really luxurious brollies, of ivory. This can be decorated in many ways.

CHAPTER NINE

The Umbrella Curated

The only major museum in the world wholly devoted to umbrellas and parasols is the Museo dell'Ombrello e del Parasole at Gignese in northern Italy, not far from Milan. It opened in one room above a school in 1939 but transferred to its present site, purpose-built in the shape of three interlocking umbrellas, in 1976. The museum is supported by Zaverio Guidetti, an umbrella-manufacturer in nearby Novara, who is its current president. It houses about 1500 examples of umbrellas and parasols, dating from the early Middle Ages to the present. Some are rare and costly specimens of silk and silver thread, some are of wool, alpaca or leather, some – the most recent examples – are synthetic.

On the ground floor about 150 parasols and umbrellas are displayed to demonstrate the changes in brolly and parasol fashions from the 17th century to the present. The first floor is dedicated to the history of the region's umbrella-makers. Many, born into poor families, were sent away very young to train as apprentices before they started up on their own. Later some returned to settle in Gignese, bringing their wives, children and money back home. There were once about 180 umbrella-making families in the towns and villages around. Several of these, the so-called pioneers, took their businesses across Europe and to North and South America.

In the USA there is another, far smaller museum run on very different lines. The Umbrella Cover Museum in Peaks Island, Maine celebrates umbrella covers. The collection was created and is curated by Nancy Hoffman, who has collected more than 600 umbrella covers

A woman walking a terrier dog flirts with a man she has just passed via the erotic magic of her parasol. From a trade card c.1880 advertising Falkner's Fine Hats in Utica, New York.

from 30 countries. The Umbrella Cover Museum is 'dedicated to the appreciation of the mundane in everyday life. It is about finding wonder and beauty in the simplest of things, and about knowing that there is always a story behind the cover.' Nancy Hoffman had the idea for the museum when she was clearing out a closet and discovered seven umbrella covers. The museum started in her kitchen, being moved to a larger location as the collection grew. The museum's collection ranges in size from a two-and-a-half-inch Barbie Doll cover to a six-foot (1.90m) patio umbrella sleeve. It has also hosted special exhibitions including 'People and Their Covers' and 'New Umbrella Cover Fashions'. The museum is open only in the summer half of the year. On her guided tours Nancy, who is also a musician, sings *Let a Smile Be Your Umbrella* while playing an accordion.

One of the more unusual variants James Smith offers its clients is having their umbrella handles carved in the form of their favourite pets.

CHAPTER TEN

Around the World:
Famed Umbrella-Makers of Today

While most umbrellas today are mass-produced in China – Shangyu city southwest of Shanghai has more than 1,000 factories making parasols and umbrellas of all types – there remain individual bespoke or boutique umbrella-makers around the world. Some, such as James Smith and Swaine Adeney Brigg, both in London, have been in existence for centuries. Others, such as the San Francisco Umbrella Company or Heurtault in Paris, are new, having been founded only in the last few years. All, however, are dedicated to making or selling umbrellas that are beautiful, durable and usable.

Swaine Adeney Brigg, the oldest British umbrella-makers, date back to the 18th century, although they only assumed the present triple form in 1943 when Brigg & Sons joined the other two. Their brolly-making skills were recognised in 1893 when they received a Royal Warrant from Queen Victoria. They also supply hats and accessories to other sorts of royalty.

In 1980 Stephen Spielberg and Harrison Ford entered the shop in St James's, London, in search of what would become the iconic hat of Indiana Jones: the brown felt 'Poet's Hat'. And for James Bond in *From Russia with Love* Swaine Adeney Brigg supplied an attaché case complete with secret compartments for ammunition, gold coins, knives and a folding rifle. A more conventional attaché case can be ordered these days. Among their designs is the Malacca Flask umbrella, with a screw-in drinking flask in the cane handle. All umbrellas from Swaine Adeney Brigg are still hand-made in their Cambridge workshops.

An old *Boursier* or bag-maker's shop as portrayed in Diderot's original
Encyclopédie published between 1751 and 1772. These craftsmen were also
skilled umbrella-makers, who developed techniques still used by their most

dedicated and traditionalist descendants. *Fig. 1* shows a worker cutting out lengths of brass with which to make the ribs of the umbrella. *Fig. 2* shows the other worker sewing the canopy together.

The oldest and most atmospheric umbrella emporium in the world is James Smith in New Oxford Street, London. Umbrellas, like walking sticks, are still made to measure in workshops directly beneath the shop.

James Smith and Sons, the second most venerable British umbrella-maker, opened its first shop in 1830 at Foubert Place in Mayfair in central London. It later moved to its present colourful premises in New Oxford Street – a gem of Victoriana – where umbrellas are still made beneath the shop. This allows customers to have alterations made at the very last minute to bespoke brollies if they wish.

James Smith was among the pioneers of the new steel Fox frame in the mid-19th century and has continued to develop new materials and techniques since. For a long time it made more walking-sticks and

...an umbrellas, because for a long time such sticks were thought ... part of a gentleman's outfit. To this day many discerning ... their canes or walking sticks from James Smith.

... of fine umbrellas, Charles Henry Wolfenbloode of ... Standards Commission, has expressed a ... umbrellas over those of Swaine Adeney Brigg, ... same shopping spree. The Smith umbrella he ... found elegant, surprisingly light and 'easy to furl and ... . Wolfenbloode has four umbrellas, one for each season. Many ... ents of James Smith own far more. An interesting James Smith variant is their range of ladies' umbrellas with distinctive carved animal heads: parrot, duck, spaniel, greyhound, fox, cat...

Another globally renowned British umbrella-makers is Fox's Umbrellas. In 1868 Mr Thomas Fox opened a shop in the City of London making and selling umbrellas. Through various changes of ownership and location Fox's has continued to make umbrellas of excellent quality. All their umbrellas are still hand made in Croydon, south London, in workshops to which they moved in 2006. They supply umbrellas to famous retailers such as Ralph Lauren, Alfred Dunhill, Fortnum & Mason, Hackett, Harrods and Turnbull & Asser in Britain; Mitsukoshi, Isetan, Sogo and Tomorrowland in Japan; Paul Stuart, Rain or Shine and Barneys in New York, plus other establishments around the world. Fox's customers have also included the British and Japanese royal families and President J.F. Kennedy. John Steed's dashing umbrellas in the 1960s series *The Avengers* came from Fox's.

In Paris the most illustrious newcomer to deluxe umbrella-making is Michel Heurtault. Calling himself 'an artisan in a constant quest for perfection, guided by the desire of restoring umbrellas and parasols to their former glory', Heurtault looks for inspiration to Impressionist paintings and 19th-century French literature. Some of his parasols

A new-established Parisian umbrella-maker of excellence, Michel Heurtault calls himself 'an artisan in a constant quest for perfection, guided by the desire of restoring umbrellas and parasols to their former glory'. He makes some umbrellas himself.

bear the names of renowned seaside resorts of that era: Deauville, Trouville, Biarritz and Brighton. His men's umbrellas often have English-sounding names: Justin, Charles, Ferdinand and, significantly, Steed. Heurtault opened his shop on the Avenue Daumesnil, Paris in 2008, and in 2011 Maison Heurtault was awarded the EPV (Living Heritage Companies), official recognition of his continuation of the centuries-old Parisian tradition of craftsmanship. His umbrellas and parasols are all hand-made in his Paris workshops using very traditional skills. Some cutting tools are 200 years old.

In Milan, Paris's great fashion rival, superb umbrellas and parasols are sold by two very different companies. Francesco Maglia, the doyen of Italian umbrella-making, was founded in 1850 and is now in its fifth generation of the same family owners. Priding themselves on following the classic *linea inglese* in both 'country' and modish metropolitan styles, they produce a huge range of umbrellas. These include some with marvellously colourful covers in tartan, pinstripe and jacquard, and with handles of wood, leather, mother-of-pearl or gilded horn. Unusually, Francesco Maglia offers umbrellas of varying lengths, with sticks from 21 to 30 inches long (52 to 75cm), and with either eight or ten ribs.

Pasotti is a far younger company. It was founded in 1956 by Ernesta Pasotti, mother of the present proprietor Eva Giacomini. Ernesta Pasotti sold 'one of a kind' umbrellas, riding around on her

A snapshot of Maglia's beautiful range. The *linea inglese* is an homage to Britain's importance in developing the concept of the modern umbrella...or it may simply be a continental jibe at British weather. Of particular note are the exquisitely crafted handles emblazoned with the maker's seal.

scooter to deliver them directly to customers. Pasotti grew into a large business at one stage before shrinking back – in the face of mass competition – to a small company whose umbrellas are specially made near Mantua. With many different designs, styles and handles, and with trimmings that can include Swarovski crystals, Pasotti makes 30,000 very distinctive umbrellas a year: These are sold in selective brollerias in 55 countries around the world.

One noted and long-established emporium of umbrellas is Rain or Shine Umbrellas in central Manhattan. It sells a huge range of umbrellas and sunshades along with walking sticks from suppliers around the world to the discerning New Yorker. The discerning north Californian until recently was not so well served, however.

Then in February 2011 Marc Brown, wandering the streets of San Francisco, discovered that many local shops and stores had run out of umbrellas while 'the rains, that had begun in early November,

One of the newer Milanese umbrella-makers is Pasotti, whose range can be startlingly original.

continued to fall every day'. Talking to shopkeepers, he realised that there was no well-reputed boutique umbrella company in or near San Francisco. He began researching the umbrella business, first visiting China to see if there was an opening for a Californian company committed to designing and selling beautiful, functional umbrellas. From his researches sprang the San Francisco Umbrella Company.

'In Europe and Japan there are boutique manufacturers of umbrellas...guided by the highest principals', he explains. 'We intend to emulate their commitment to their products and to their customers. It is very sad to say but true that many Americans hate their umbrellas...because they break so easily... [and] are unattractive and often cheap and shoddy. [But] umbrellas can be beautiful and functional and can last a lifetime if proper materials are used in their construction and proper care taken in design and execution. That is the mission of The San Francisco Umbrella Company.' With such a ringing declaration of faith, the umbrella and parasol look set to thrive in the third millennium.

The unhappy consequences of being caught in a storm. Etiquette demands that the umbrella be left at home in favour of good headwear on a windy day, though these gentlemen's top hats seem to fare little better.

CHAPTER ELEVEN

Umbrella Etiquette

An umbrella should *never* be opened inside a house, as every brolly-user knows or ought to know. To do supposedly brings bad luck. It can certainly bring in rain, dousing homes and shops with sudden showers. For while you, thanks to your brolly, may not be wet, your umbrella certainly is. But even when opened outside on the street, an umbrella vastly expands your 'personal space' on crowded city pavements. Worse, if held up against the wind and rain – as it often is – it can blind you to what is happening just in front. While you are cosily sheltered against the elements, your umbrella may be poking into other people's faces, threatening to stab, even to blind them, with its steel tip. And on public transport, whether bus, trains, cable-cars or vaporetti (it rains in Venice too, heavily), if hung over the back of the seat in front it will dig into the passenger just ahead and make other seats wet. (The traditional Englishman unfurled his umbrella only in the most pressing circumstances for just such reasons – see Winston Churchill and Lloyd George on page 56).

Because of all this, attempts are now being made around the world – in New York, San Francisco, Singapore and Sydney as well as in London, Rome and Paris – to introduce a global etiquette for umbrellas. Among the suggested guidelines are:

Get an umbrella of the right size both for you physically and for the place where you will be using it. A huge golf umbrella is far too big for city boulevards and pavements, and if you are a small person it can look ridiculous on you anyway.

When opening an umbrella outside, look around first and then hold it directly above you so that it does not open horizontally. This is particularly important if your umbrella is an automatic and can *explode* in front of others when you press a button.

On passing someone, do not tilt your brolly to one side. This leaves you exposed to rain and may let water drip onto your shoulders or someone else's. Rather, lower your umbrella if you are shorter than the other; if you are taller, raise it. This action has been called the Dance of the Umbrellas, in which (ideally) umbrellas dance along the street in choreographed harmony. And always be aware of other people's eyes.

Under scaffolding, close your umbrella unless there is no one else within umbrella poke. There is a serious shortage of head room beneath most scaffolding.

When entering a building, close your umbrella after tapping its end on the ground outside to remove excessive water. Keep it closed and do not attempt to dry it off by repeatedly opening and closing it. If there is no proper umbrella stand – and these days such an essential is often lacking – lean it tip-down against a convenient wall or, if in a public place, put it under your seat. Wherever you put it, make certain that your umbrella cannot trip up a passer-by.

Never cause or succumb to Umbrella Rage. Walking three abreast with friends, all with umbrellas held high, effectively means you have taken over the pavement. Don't do it. It will cause offence. So will carrying your furled umbrella horizontally like a sword. Point it down at the ground.

Lastly: hard though it is to admit, there are days – very windy days, normally – when umbrellas simply are not appropriate. Use a good raincoat and hat in such tempests and leave your umbrella at home.

The umbrella's decorative importance has not been lost on the food and drink industry as a symbol of the exotic, standing proudly atop a fruity dessert or floating languidly in a cocktail.

Lost and Not Found

> 'The rain it raineth everyday
> On the just and the unjust fella;
> But mainly on the just because
> The unjust steals the just's umbrella.'
> Samuel Butler 1835-1902 (attrib.)

The Mystery of the Missing Umbrella might have baffled Sherlock Holmes if he had turned his mind to it. No object is lost or forgotten more often. Easy to leave behind – in restaurant, shop, train or hotel – the umbrella is also frequently taken by others. This may be an inadvertent purloining by honest strangers who fail to realise that this particular brolly is not theirs. (The problem is worse for the male brolly-bearer than the female, as most men's umbrellas look so alike i.e. black.) But there is undoubtedly a larcenous minority who simply steal other people's brollies.

Hilaire Beloc, the pugnacious novelist, was about to leave his club one rainy day when he discovered that his umbrella was missing. Incensed, he put up a notice saying: 'Would the nobleman who took my umbrella please return it?' Perplexed, his friends asked why he was so certain that a *nobleman* had taken it. 'Because no gentleman would take another man's umbrella!' he replied determinedly. Belloc was possibly wrong in this instance, but he was fortunate to get his brolly back. Most people who lose umbrellas do not. Having your name and address carved on the handle may help the honest to return your lost umbrella to you, but it also adds to its cost. A cheaper option is to tape your name on a piece of paper to the handle, although this is easily washed off by rain. Hanging on to your brolly demands perpetual vigilance. But it pays off when it rains.